Brigid McConville

The Role of Trade Unions

Macdonald

A MACDONALD BOOK

© Brigid McConville, 1986

First published in Great Britain in 1986 by
Macdonald & Co. (Publishers) Ltd
London and Sydney
A BPCC plc company

ISBN 0 356 11619 0

Editor Donna Bailey
Production Controller Rosemary Bishop
Picture Research Elizabeth Loving

Printed in Great Britain by
Purnell Book Production Ltd
Member of the BPCC Group

Macdonald & Co. (Publishers) Ltd
Greater London House
Hampstead Road
London NW1 7QX

BRITISH LIBRARY
CATALOGUING IN PUBLICATION DATA

McConville, Brigid
    The role of trade unions. – (Debates)
    1.Trade-unions
    I.Title   II. Series
    331.88   HD 6483
    ISBN 0-356-11619-0

Contents

What is a

A
ll manner of working people today belong to trade unions, whether employed or unemployed, from doctors to dockers, school teachers to secretaries, pilots to printers. A union card is carried by more people than a cheque card or credit card.

With no union to protect them, these Brazilian electronics workers toil long hours in cramped conditions.

Today's trade unions have reached a critical point in their history. Should their powers be curbed by government legislation, or should they be strengthened as the representatives of working people's rights? In a time of recession and high unemployment, especially amongst young people, this question is central to our future.

Matters of dispute The role of trade unions is hotly disputed. Those who support them say that they are the only defence that the average worker has against the power of the State and employers to cut wages, sack workers or impose harsh conditions. Trade unions claim to put people before profit, keeping human values alive in an increasingly cruel and competitive world. They claim to stand for freedom, democracy and social justice.

Those who argue against trade unions say that they abuse their powers to demand unfairly high wages and they hold their employers – and the general public – to ransom with the threat of strikes. Their detractors argue that unions are undemocratic, out of touch with their members and dominated by 'bully-boys'. Unions they say, have a 'stranglehold' on industry; that through closed shops they keep non-union people out of work, and that unions may use their power to bring about social change, the fall of governments, or even revolution.

> 'We … question a system which dictates that the will of a handful of people can be imposed on the wishes of a great many.'
> Norman Tebbit, 1983

trade union?

> 'Unions don't just represent the people of Britain. They are the people of Britain.'
>
> Len Murray, former Gen. Sec. of TGWU in
> Hands Up For Democracy, 1983

Strength in numbers? A trade union is a group (or 'union') of working people who are all employees rather than employers. They also generally have in common a 'trade' – or a skill, occupation or simply the same employer.

The union is run and paid for by its members to protect and promote their interests. It makes its voice heard through the process of collective bargaining, on the basis that a boss is more likely to listen to the united point of view of the workers than to a lone and vulnerable individual. If a boss ignores this voice, the group can take collective action to back up their claims.

Ninety per cent of unions are affiliated to the Trades Union Congress (TUC). Sometimes a 'breakaway' union forms over differences of opinion (like the Union of Democratic Miners which split from the NUM), or the TUC will consider suspending or expelling a union which is out of step (like the electricians in the Wapping printing dispute).

Since the Employment Act of 1980, when legal procedures for union recognition were scrapped, workers must negotiate or use industrial action or conciliation procedures if an employer will not recognize their organization.

People of all kinds support the health service workers in this trade union mass rally at Hammersmith.

Early days

The origins of the trade union movement are closely linked to the beginning of modern industrialized society. In the history of their joint development can be seen many of the patterns – of conflict and cooperation – that still exist today.

Roots Trade unions as we know them date back to the first workers' clubs and societies of the late 17th century, but the term 'union' wasn't used until the early 1900s. They were born out of often intolerable conditions, poverty and squalor. It was a period when employers exacted a working day of up to 18 hours, when wages were barely enough for survival in comfortless and insanitary conditions, and when children were often forced to work as soon as they could walk.

Until the late 19th century, few working men – and no women – could vote, and so they had no say in how things were run. The ruling classes and employers who elected the government generally showed little concern for the lives of manual workers and suppressed any signs of discontent.

Trade unions grew as a workers' defence against appalling exploitation, as in this Victorian tailors' sweatshop in London.

However, as the medieval system of journeymen's gilds had fallen into decay with the growth of industry, more and more tradesmen 'combined' to protect their interests – in spite of the laws against such 'combinations'. The first well known example of such an organization to raise wages is that of the journeymen feltmakers. In 1696 they sent a delegation to negotiate with their employers, and several were prosecuted as a result. Then in the 1720s, the master tailors of London had cause to complain that their journeymen 'to the number of 7,000 (had) entered into a combination to raise their wages and leave off working an hour sooner.'

As industry spread and prices rose, combinations proved impossible to suppress. But the 1780s and 1790s were a time of revolution and risings abroad, and at the end of the century, Parliament made new laws against the combinations. Yet in trades where the jobs of skilled artisans were at risk from the new machinery, frustration broke out into violence as the 'Luddites' organized systematic breaking of machines from 1812 to 1814. They were named after Ned Ludd, the signatory of an agreement that the Nottingham workers intended to 'break and destroy' machinery in the lace trade.

The nucleus emerges Luddism spread to the countryside as the Napoleonic Wars came to an end in 1815, a time of further poverty and concern for 'public order'. Then in 1819 came 'Peterloo' when eleven peaceful demonstrators in Manchester were massacred by a charge of the Yeomanry. The 'Six Acts' followed to curb demonstrations and public meetings, and it was not for another three years that the fear of revolution ebbed enough for Parliament to change the laws.

It was in 1824 that the Act against combinations was finally repealed, allowing working class organizations to grow as a recognized part of society. Yet it was not until 1871 that unions won the right to strike without their funds being put at risk – a right which some say is now being reversed.

Governments have long used the laws to curb union strength, as in this 1927 Punch cartoon of Mr Baldwin trying to put a legal 'collar' on the unionist watchdog.

> 'The selfishness of workers in attempting to secure better conditions at the cost of rising unemployment and immense public misery can be just as morally indefensible as the rapaciousness of the wealthy in exploiting the working class.'
> The Chief Rabbi, Sir Immanuel Jakobovits in the Guardian, 1986

One for all?

The 1920s and 30s were both a time of depression and a period of union growth. Faced with this conflict, the government intervened to curb union power by backing the employers' bid to cut miners' wages in 1926. In response the TUC called for co-ordinated action, and industry came to a halt in the General Strike. After nine days the TUC called it off. The consciousness of trade unionists about what they could achieve together had been altered forever, but the immediate defeat was not to be overcome until the election of the first Labour Government in 1945.

Changing with the times Historically, British unions have grown where they were needed, with different organizations for skilled (crafts) and unskilled labour. Hence our 'multi-union' system where many different unions may operate within one workplace. Its critics say that our system has failed to change with the times, and that the old structures impede technological progress through the unions' unwillingness to adapt to new styles of work.

UK unions are sometimes unfavourably compared to those of Japan and Germany who both created purpose-built, streamlined trade unions and a fresh industrial base when they started from scratch in the aftermath of the war. Nor do these countries suffer so much from the old 'them and us' attitudes of class conflict which persist in the thinking of both workers and management in Britain. Some say such attitudes are a relic of the past; others say class conflict is still a present day reality.

Critics also point to the regional union 'barons' whose power is based on personality and local strength. Such leaders kept unions alive in the teeth of opposition from the often ruthless bosses of the past. However, they say, the pattern persists to cause

rivalry and competition for members between unions. The argument is that this encourages union bosses to look to their immediate advantage in winning recruits rather than long term strategies; rivalry may keep the cost of contributions down, but it also depletes funds and puts huge pressure on union officials.

Right In a massive show of solidarity, British workers defied the government during the 1926 General Strike.

German workers in this Cologne tractor factory belong to a trade union movement which – since the Second World War – has been rebuilt on a streamlined model.

Mergers versus multinationals Yet British unions have made progress in reducing their original fragmentation. In 1986 there were 96 British unions with about 11 million members, half as many as after the war and with 30 per cent more members, but still far more cumbersome than West Germany however, with a main union centre of 19 unions for over 7 million workers.

Arguably, the mergers of unions have been a necessary survival response to the enormous power of the multinational companies, which have been dubbed 'the new colonists'. Some oil companies are richer than some European countries, and it is said that Ford (UK) was able to fix its profits in the UK downwards as a strategy to strengthen its hand in bargaining with the trade unions. Against such opposition, say unionists, the fewer – and the stronger – they are, the better.

Power for

Unions are based on the principle of strength in numbers. But the bigger they get, the more their detractors accuse them

> 'The TUC huffs and puffs as though it speaks for millions. The reality is that it speaks for only thousands of committed activists and nothing more.'
>
> SDP Policy Document no. 8, 1985

of not representing the views of the individual member. Is this true, or is it a hypocritical attack from enemies of the unions who are themselves undemocratic?

Making decisions Union members belong to branches, and at branch meetings they can have a say in the activities and running of the union. Some people say they are put off even at this stage by the formality or inconvenience of meetings, and that this leaves motivated 'extremists' or 'activists' to take over. Others say we all have an equal opportunity to be 'activists'.

Members elect their own branch secretary, chairperson and committee. They also choose delegates to attend the union's annual national conference. This conference usually elects a National Executive, a committee which acts on behalf of all the members.

Decisions may be made in the workplace through 'collective bargaining', when issues like wages are discussed between the union and the employer. After both sides argue their case, a compromise is usually reached. The Executive of the union can negotiate a National Agreement – like a

The TUC, representing most trade unionists, gathers in an annual Congress to debate and express the views of working people.

the masses?

national wage claim – on behalf of the whole of their membership.

The role of the TUC Nine out of ten unionists and all the major unions belong to the Trade Union Congress or TUC. Based at Congress House in London, the TUC puts forward the collective view of the trade union movement on a wide range of issues from the economy, education, health and social policy to international affairs. The TUC's annual Congress is attended by over a thousand delegates representing the affiliated unions who decide its overall policy. The TUC has a General Council of over 50 members including a General Secretary, to carry out the decisions of Congress and provide leadership. The chief job of the TUC is to put the trade unions' point of view on issues which come up for de-cision by the government. It also presides over any disputes which might occur between unions, as well as running education and training courses for trade unionists.

The TUC has been dubbed the trade union 'carthorse', to suggest that it may be strong but it is also slow and plodding. Indeed the whole trade union system is at times accused of being a lumbering impediment to the freedom of business. Managers sometimes complain that unions are more interested in maintaining the *status quo* and defending their pay packets than in increasing productivity or responding to the challenge of new technology. The government measures of the 80s have gone a long way to curb union powers, but the unions say it is themselves, and not the government, who are the genuine and democratic voice of working people.

Sunderland shipyard workers at the end of a shift: there have been fears that privatisation could mean the end of their jobs.

Reds under

'Trade unions must become the founder of the new society. The Socialist revolution can only be accomplished by the . . . collaboration of millions of individuals. The trade unions must educate the masses and lead them to share in the government of the country.'
Nikolai Lenin, head of Soviet State, 1919

In the Red corner . . . Trade unions or their precursors were around long before Karl Marx, but his theories as to their role are still influential. Marxists see the revolutionary overthrow of capitalism as the inevitable consequence of a basic conflict between the working classes and capitalist bosses. To Marx, winning gains in wages and conditions seemed less important than the function of trade unions in developing class consciousness, so helping to provide centres of resistance to capitalism.

Much of current socialist thinking, a 'revisionist' strain of Marxism, aims for the rejection of capitalism for a more just social order. But rather than revolution, it sees Parliament as the chief instrument of change. In much of Western Europe, the trade union movement has joined forces with the socialist political parties to participate in 'social democracy'. But to some left wing thinkers this is a sell-out. They say that when trade unions collaborate with the establishment, they become a tool for suppressing the just demands of the working class.

In the Blue corner . . . Some capitalists see trade unions as necessary for efficient planning of the economy. They argue that the capitalist state needs the consent of the workforce as represented by unions, and that the union role in educating the workforce and negotiating for them helps business to develop. However, some capitalist thinkers are fundamentally hostile to the role of trade unions, and blame them for unemployment, stagnation and strikes. They say unions push prices up, hamper the 'free market' and slow the adjustment of the economy to new technology.

the beds?

And in the real world . . . By and large the capitalist West has accommodated (some would say diluted) the power of unions to its own needs. In many right wing and totalitarian countries however, unions are still banned as revolutionary, unionists are forced to operate underground and many are imprisoned, tortured and killed, as in some Latin American countries and South Africa. In Russia and Soviet controlled countries, the role of unions is mainly to support government planners and to help meet production targets. Soviet unions also sponsor social and cultural activities and organize benefits for workers, like holidays and sick pay. But the bargaining power of these unions tends to be less than those of the West, and the government decides wages

> *'These (the British Government's trade union laws) are the kinds of laws that you find in places like Argentina, Guatemala and Poland. And we know what 'freedom' means in those countries.'*
> TUC publication Hands Up for Democracy, *1983*

and working hours, while strikes are illegal. Some Soviet unionists have been imprisoned as dissidents.

There are trade unionists in the UK who fear that the government's new laws are reducing British unions to the same level.

Opposite Karl Marx is the father of modern socialism and his theory of workers' revolution still has worldwide influence.

There are no free trade unions in the USSR, where dissident workers are imprisoned in this kind of 'labour camp'.

Whose right

It often seems as if management and trade unions are speaking (or not speaking) across a great divide. The unions claim to represent 'human values' in protecting the interest of their members – like their right to jobs for a fair wage. Some unionists believe they should have a say in major decisions and strategies like cuts in the workforce, investment and corporate planning. For their part, managements today generally concede that management should be 'by consent of the employed' with regard to issues like holidays, wages and hours.

> 'The evils visited upon the working population by employers during the Industrial Revolution left a legacy of hostility which management inherited.'
> Cooper and Bartlett in Industrial Relations, 1976

Right Workers rarely have a say in how companies are run, while management make the key decisions – for better or for worse.

When disagreements arise however, they tend to insist on their 'right to manage' and keep sole control of major decisions.

Managers often say that the harsh economic realities of competition and recession make it necessary for them to close plants and sack workers. Ultimately, they are responsible to an employer in the task of maximising efficiency, increasing productivity and reducing costs. They reject the image of themselves as putting profits before people by arguing that they are creating wealth for the whole community.

Them and us As with so many aspects of industrial relations in Britain, history reveals much about current conflict. It was the early factory system which created a class of employees who based their authority on expertise. They were not the owners, but they acted in the owners' interests, and behaved with as little concern for the welfare of the other workers. These 'managers' were also better paid and more privileged, and quickly were identified as 'them' as opposed to 'us' from the workers' point of view. Today the terms 'owner' and 'management' still tend to be used interchangeably and much of the old hostility persists.

In their recent survey of business people, the management organization, the CBI, observed that negative social attitudes are one of the UK's main weaknesses, especially

to manage?

the 'them and us' divide. They pointed out however that it is an attitude which 'is found in management just as much as in employees.'

Cooperation – or collaboration? Yet management and unions are certainly not always in conflict. Today's managers generally recognize that employees' involvement in the affairs of a firm improve its competitiveness and raise profits. Workers for their part recognize that successful management can mean job security and better pay. The number of incentive schemes which offer profit-sharing and share ownership to employees has doubled in the last five years. Most disputes are settled without strikes, which are at their lowest level for many years.

On a nation-wide level, management and unions also have a constructive working relationship through their joint membership of such bodies as the Health and Safety Commission, the arbitration board ACAS, the Manpower Services Commission, the Commission for Racial Equality, the National Economic Development Council and the Equal Opportunities Commission.

These shop stewards represent Rosyth workers in the TGWU; it is their job to put to management the workers' demands and grievances.

> '*Relationships between workers and employers have to be based on agreement and consent, not on instructions given from above.*'
> Jack Jones, former Gen. Sec. of TGWU, 1977

Politics and

Mutual hostility has often been the norm between unionists and the business establishment, but here, the controversial and conservative electricians' leader Eric Hammond speaks to the CBI Conference.

The traditional antagonism between governments – especially Conservative ones – and trade unions is still as sharp as ever, with each claiming that the other is out to destroy them. Some would say that the problems arise from a real conflict of interest: power for the ruling elite versus power for the mass of working people. Others believe that in a democracy, there is no reason why both sides shouldn't co-operate, apart from outmoded 'class conflict' politics and intransigence.

'Mrs Thatcher and her friends go on about freedom . . . But their kind of freedom is the freedom of the employer to pay sweated wages (and there are still plenty who do that) and the right of the hungry person to starve.'
Len Murray in Hands Up For Democracy, 1983

A question of restraint? Since the war, governments have tried various methods of 'wage restraint' in an attempt to control rising prices and rising earnings. The 1950s and early 60s saw several attempts by Tory governments to limit salary increases, which met with union rejection. It was not until the 1964 Labour government that some unions became more willing to accept an incomes policy and took their place on a Prices and Incomes Board with business representatives. In the long run it was not a successful strategy – hardly surprising to those who saw unions as created to improve their members' pay, rather than to control their members' aspirations for better wages.

My boss, the Government . . . The government is a major employer across the whole spectrum of work, including transport, the docks, education, and social services. The NHS is the single largest employer in the country. As such the Tories have come into continuing conflict with the trade unions, who insist both that public spending and wages in these sectors is too low. Recent years have seen unprecedented and long term strikes by nurses and teachers against cuts and low pay. Of course, the unions don't negotiate directly with the government in these cases, but with managers and negotiators appointed by them through the civil service. Sometimes, as with the appointment of Ian McGregor to head British Steel and then the Coal Board, the unions accuse the government of using a 'hatchet man' to make the cuts it wants.

During the 70s, the trade union movement proved it had the power to bring the government to a halt, as it did in the miners' strike which brought down Ted Heath's administration. Since then however, the Tories have brought in a series of laws which they say are aimed at curbing union abuses of power.

'If the trade union movement is allowed to carry on, on this course of self-destruction, then Britain will slide further into the trough and the people who will suffer most are our workers and their families.'

Tom Peet, Director of Conservative Trade Unionists, 1985

The two Employment Acts and the Trade Union Acts have weakened the closed shop, obliged unions to ballot members in disputes, and have restricted the traditional right of unionists to take action in support of members of other unions. Under these laws, the miners and the print workers have been heavily fined and had their assets taken over by the courts. Government employees at Cheltenham GCHQ, the intelligence gathering centre, have been told that for reasons of national security they are not permitted to belong to a trade union.

Trade unionists, on the other hand, have accused the Tories of a cynical attempt to cripple British trade unions which (unlike those of European countries) rely on hard-won practice rather than rights enshrined in law.

NUM leaders arrive at No.10 for talks with Labour Prime Minister Callaghan – not a likely event under a Tory government.

A question of

Labour governments have traditionally been far more in harmony with the trade union movement than have the Conservatives. The Labour Party itself was born of the trade union movement at the turn of the century, and many of the laws which protected the rights of workers were brought

> 'The trade unions created their own party, the Labour party, because other parties did not want the trade unions to be represented in Parliament. It is only through the Labour Party that we are able to take part in making policies about the future of our industry and services.'
>
> *TGWU publication*
> Why and How we Should Keep the Fund, *1985*

in under Labour during the 1970s. However, not everything in the Labour movement garden has been rosy, as the Labour Party's leadership's reluctance to support Arthur Scargill in the latest miners' strike has shown.

The cost of comradeship Before the first World War, financial support of the Labour Party by trade unions was legalized. Those who didn't wish to pay this 'political levy' could 'contract out' or choose not to contribute to the fund. This was changed to 'contracting in' after the General Strike of 1926, making it necessary for individual unionists to positively express a wish to contribute.

The system was changed back to 'contracting out' by the 1945 Labour Government. The latest Tory Government has also moved to scrap the fund, but with little success. For their part, the unions point

out that all other organizations – like big business – can spend what they like on political activity without government interference.

The unions' political funds are also used to sponsor candidates in the Labour Party who are running for local council office and for Parliament. They say it is essential to have a voice inside Parliament to influence decisions made there on issues like job security, pay, pensions and wages. Many unions work to persuade the Labour Party to take up their own policies which they hope will be put into action by a Labour Government. For these reasons too, many unions 'affiliate' to the Labour Party.

representation

The true voice of Labour? This system has been attacked by Tories, Liberals and the SDP alike, who say it is not fair to the many unionists who don't vote Labour. They claim it makes trade unions into the real, but unelected voice of the Labour Party. But the unions argue that employers and other organizations also make sure they have MPs who speak up for their interest in Parliament. They point out that as consumers, we all pay a great deal more into the profits of companies than we do into union funds, yet we can't stop our money being used by companies to finance political (usually Conservative) donations.

After their election victory in 1982, the Tories claimed that the traditional support of the working class for Labour had been broken. They believe that today's prosperous Britons were more interested in individual advancement – through buying their own council houses for instance – than in 'old fashioned' class based politics. A survey in 1983 showed that two-thirds of the country's biggest union, the TGWU, didn't vote Labour, and Conservatives said that 40 per cent of unionists supported their policies.

Since then however, most unions have been balloted on whether or not they want to keep a political fund. Against government predictions, so far 80 per cent have voted to keep the fund.

The trade union movement has strong links with the Labour Party, although Neil Kinnock did not fully support Arthur Scargill during the miners' strike.

Who are the workers anyway?

Like the trade unions, employers' associations in Britain were formed in response to circumstances – such as strikes by workers. The Combination Acts (which banned workers' associations) were not used against the employers, and until the First World War, when the government took over their initiative, employers' associations often set the pace in industrial relations.

The employers' TUC? These days the chief employers' grouping is the Confederation of British Industry (CBI) which is seen as the voice of industrialists and manufacturers. It includes companies large and small, private and public, employers and trades associations. Just as employers' associations are seen as parallel to the unions in their function, the CBI is regarded as the equivalent of the TUC. The CBI even claims to represent more workers than the TUC, as its affiliated employers cover some three-quarters of the workforce.

Unlike the TUC, the CBI cannot intervene in disputes which affect its members – it can only offer advice. Loss of CBI membership would not be as damaging to a firm as loss of TUC membership to a trade union. The CBI's primary job is to represent the employers' point of view to the government, the public and the unions. The CBI is anxious not to appear hostile to trade unions. They acknowledge the influence of unions on the workplace, and say they want 'positive change' which (to them) includes the recent 'reform' of the laws. Electricians' leader Eric Hammond, who proclaims himself a 'realist', has spoken at the CBI Conference. But many unionists see this as a 'sell out', collaborating in the control of workers by management.

Employers' militant tendency? Other notable employers' associations which act as powerful pressure groups include the Chambers of Commerce which are powerful at a local level, and the Institute of Directors (IoD), which has become a strong pressure group for Conservative ideas in recent years. The IoD, with its demands for government legislation to curb union powers, has been likened to the 'militant tendency' of the bosses in its extreme attitudes.

Blurring of distinctions The division between employers and workers is not always clear cut however. Many senior workers have a management role. In recent years too, the membership of 'white collar' unions has increased enormously as non-manual and professional people seek to protect their jobs. Their unions are often concerned with maintaining 'differentials' – the gaps in pay between various categories of worker. Increasingly with the spread of new technology, these distinctions are becoming blurred.

> *'A company whose managers fail to manage, where decision makers fail to take decisions will not provide secure employment (or anything else) for long.'*
>
> CBI document Change to Succeed, *1985*

'We advocate free enterprise because it is more effective in creating wealth than collectivism and is the best guarantee of personal freedom.'

CBI document
Change to Succeed, 1985

Anatomy of a strike

Below The year long miners' strike mobilized support from all sectors of the Labour movement who felt themselves under attack from Thatcherism.

The miners' strike of 1984–85 is said to have changed the face of the British labour movement. Thousands of miners went on strike for 12 months in opposition to the Coal Board's plan to close pits. They came into daily and often violent conflict with the government, police and working miners in a struggle which many believed was about more than jobs for miners.

The government and Coal Board's Ian McGregor argued that uneconomical pits must be closed, and accused the miners of violence and mass intimidation. During the strike there were some nine thousand arrests and two miners were killed on picket lines. The NUM's funds were sequestered and the leader of Kent NUM imprisoned.

While the rank and file of the labour movement overwhelmingly gave their support, raising millions of pounds in collections, trade union and labour leaders were not always willing to back up NUM boss Arthur Scargill. The strike ended in defeat for the miners, and the NUM are still fighting to get sacked members reinstated and imprisoned members released.

> *'The miners' strike, where the leaders of the NUM have misused the rules to suit themselves, and have abused the loyalty . . . of mine-workers and their families will be remembered as the start of the move back to moderation by the movement.'*
>
> *Tom Peet in* CTU News, *1985*

A bitter legacy The government hailed the defeat of the miners as a victory for the rule of law. They believed they had broken the back of a union which had plagued Toryism for a century. Since then, they say, unionists have been more reluctant to take on the full might of the government. Many people however argued that the British state – its police, laws, judges and media – had been cynically used against the workers by a ruling class determined to crush its opponents. Civil liberties groups accused the police of brutality and misconduct. They point to evidence that the government and Coal Board planned for the strike, and say they will now sell off the profitable pits and expand the nuclear power programme.

Whose defeat? Opponents of Arthur Scargill and the miners say they have paid the price for challenging the law and refusing to take a national ballot of members. The breakaway Union of Democratic Miners has further weakened the NUM. Trade unionism, they argue, is a spent force.

The unions however, claim a great achievement in mobilizing the courage, pride and determination of miners and their supporters alike. They say the new political consciousness of the miners' wives and women who helped to sustain the strikers for so long will never be lost. They regret that the Labour and trade union leadership failed to support them completely against massive odds, yet they claim that the determination of workers remains undefeated.

Mass pickets faced massed police in often violent confrontations at Orgreave during the 1984 miners' strike.

> '*Under Mrs Thatcher (the Conservatives) determined to bring the miners to heel and, if possible, inflict a major defeat on the entire trade union and labour movement.*'
> Eric Heffer MP in Digging Deeper, 1985

Above the law?

History has left a legacy of hostility between trade unions and the law in Britain. For a long time the Combination Acts outlawed unions, and it was not until they created their own political voice – the Labour Party – in 1906, that trade unions were granted certain immunities from the law. Historically too, trade union recognition and labour regulation in Britain was built up by industrial action rather than through the law. Of all the advanced industrial countries we probably have the least degree of direct legal regulation in this respect.

Solidarity – or intimidation? Yet since 1979, when public frustration over strikes in the 'Winter of Discontent' helped bring the Conservatives to power, the Tories have brought in three Acts to regulate the unions. These Acts have curtailed the collective power of unions, have weakened the rights of employees and strengthened the rights of employers. They have been chiefly aimed to curtail picketing and the closed shop.

Right These Kent dinner ladies took their case to the High Court, claiming unfair dismissal after they were sacked for not accepting cuts in their hours and conditions.

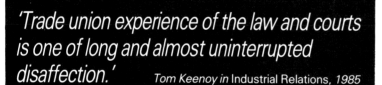

'Trade union experience of the law and courts is one of long and almost uninterrupted disaffection.'
   Tom Keenoy in Industrial Relations, *1985*

Their opponents accuse the Tories of using the courts to attack and undermine the strength of the whole trade union movement. Their supporters say union power had to be curbed, 'intimidation' by pickets had to be stopped, and that the majority of the electorate voted for these reforms.

In effect, the 1982 Employment Act has altered the law to make many kinds of strike and industrial action illegal. Strikes which are 'political', or which express 'solidarity' for other workers are now unlawful. Picketing and the right to seek sympathetic support from other unionists are limited – to such an extent that some people say it is virtually impossible to run a strike even when backed by a legally held ballot.

The new laws have also reduced the strength of the closed shop, and have changed the system to make employees prove their case if they think they have been unfairly dismissed. Workers can now be compensated if they lose their jobs for not being in the union, and unions as well as individuals are now held liable for unlawful acts, to the tune of £250,000. Unions are now also obliged to ballot their members on various issues, such as disputes, election of officers and the political fund.

Whose rights come first? British law consists of complicated – and sometimes contradictory – ideas about collective rights and individual rights. However, the courts generally put individual rights first. This means an individual can refuse to join a union even when the majority of workers have voted for a closed shop. However, individuals have no legal right to join a union in this country. On the other hand, employers are not allowed to sack striking workers unless they sack all strikers – as Mr Murdoch did in the 1986 Wapping dispute, when 5,000 printers on his 'Times International' publications came out on strike.

In recent years, legal action such as injunctions has increasingly been used against unions by employers. Judges have imposed huge fines on unions for breaking these new laws, and have sequestered union funds. Some political commentators are now suggesting that the government has gone too far in 'union bashing', and the tide of public opinion is turning again in favour of the unions.

A policeman picks up helmets after a skirmish with demonstrators outside the notorious Grunwicks film-processing plant, where management refused to recognize the clerical workers' trade union, APEX.

> *'It now seems that under British law working people don't have the right to strike, a trade union does not have the right to defend its members and a trade union has no right to call for solidarity.'* Brenda Dean, Gen. Sec. of SOGAT, 1986

The right

Trade unionists traditionally see the right to strike as the most important of fundamental union rights – even of human rights. In Britain this right was built up slowly against centuries of opposition from government and employers.

Most strikes are over wages; others are caused by a variety of issues such as working conditions. An 'official' strike is one called by a union executive, while one without executive backing is 'unofficial'.

A last resort? Trade unions say the right to strike is an essential weapon to be used in the last resort when bargaining or arbitration has broken down. However, argument still rages over whether some strikes are normally unjustifiable. Some people – unionists amongst them – believe that the right of patients to medical care should take absolute priority over the right of health workers to strike. The striking teachers have been accused of sacrificing children's

'Strikes are an aberration and occur, relatively speaking, about as frequently as plane crashes.' Tom Keenoy in Industrial Relations, *1985*

'There is nothing in this legislation which will outlaw strikes. I want a practical step by step reform of the trade unions.' James Prior, *1980*

to strike?

interests to their own. Some unionists, however, argue that unless workers in these services strike for improvements, patient care and education will both suffer more.

A question of morality? There is disagreement too over whether unions have the right to strike to force elected governments to change their economic policies – or whether strikes should be illegal in wartime. During the two World Wars there were legal restrictions on the right to strike, but stoppages took place nonetheless. Currently, the armed forces and police are forbidden to go on strike, and some would extend the ban to members in essential services such as firemen, water workers and nurses. The TUC itself believes that 'special steps have to be taken to avoid disruption to services on which the community relies'. However, they say that these should be based not on legal curbs of the right to strike, but on high standards of industrial relations.

When strikes affect the public – through stoppages of post or transport for instance – unions are often accused of being selfishly 'strike happy'. Yet unionists claim they would always prefer to avoid such action; it damages both members' incomes and union funds when strike pay has to be paid out.

Contrary to popular belief, Britain's strike record is not abysmal. Compared with many other industrialized countries, we occupy the middle ground in strikes, with far more days lost through sickness, and (the unions argue) through unemployment. Yet there is no doubt that strikes are costly to the economy. At present, say the CBI, strikes are 'at a historic low'. They have no doubt that the reason for this is the recent government legislation with its curbs on strike action. The unions, however, put this down to the slump in workers' confidence caused by unemployment, and the new laws which they say have all but destroyed their basic right to strike.

Opposite Nurses in Epsom carry water to their hospital to keep essential services going during a strike by water workers.

The government ordered that soldiers be trained to use firehoses in readiness for a threatened strike by firemen over pay.

A secret ballot?

W hen the Conservative Government came to power in 1979, it was pledged to end what it saw as the undemocratic and unrepresentative nature of trade unions. According to Conservatives, union policies were being decided by a tiny minority of left wing activists who bothered to turn up to meetings and to vote. As a result, they argued, action and strikes were begun by leaderships without the following of their members.

The NUM were attacked for not holding a ballot in the miners' strike and it was claimed that they prevented miners from going back to work by 'intimidation'. Critics also accused unionists of corruption in the case of the TGWU, which held a re-run of the disputed election for the general secretary after complaints about ballot rigging.

Extending democracy? The government used these arguments as justification for passing new laws which oblige unions to hold secret ballots on a number of issues. A closed shop must now be approved by an overwhelming majority of its members, and every voting member of a union's governing body must now be elected at least every five years by secret ballot. Furthermore, a union is now breaking the law if it takes industrial action – such as a strike – without first holding a secret ballot of its members in which a majority is in favour. Unions who wish to keep their political fund are also obliged to get their members' approval in a secret ballot at least once a decade. The government has made funds available to unions who hold such ballots by post.

Kent miners use their right to participate in union democracy by voting in a secret ballot.

> 'Never has so much been achieved against the interests of so many by so few.'
> CTU leaflet Who Speaks for You, 1985

Physician heal thyself? For their part, the unions see this as an attack on their fundamental rights and freedoms. They say they are already democratic and already use

'The unions are trapped by a measure of unfairness people never imagined when they voted for a Thatcher government to tame the unions.'

Geoffrey Goodman in the Mirror, 1986

secret ballots in many cases: all members have a voice, all officials are accountable, and indirect elections are necessary in some unions to overcome organizational complexities. The government should look to itself they say: we elect Members of Parliament, but not our Prime Minister, who stands accused of wielding autocratic power. Mr Tebbit, who framed these laws, was not elected by a postal ballot, nor was he elected into his job as Minister. The Labour Party is now pledged to give control of their own affairs back to the unions.

The laws have had their effect however, and partly through fear of legal action, more and more unions have balloted members before taking industrial action. Ironically, some managements are now complaining that such ballots have backfired, strengthening the hand of the unions when the vote is in favour of a strike! Several unions have also applied for public funds for postal ballots, and the TUC has reversed its initial rejection of this scheme, which it feared would put its freedoms into the gift of the government.

Workers at Cowley vote in a show of hands to end a strike.

In place

The first that we get to hear of an industrial dispute is generally when the media reports a strike. Yet in 99 per cent of cases, conflicting interests between employers and employees are solved without strikes, through collective bargaining. This is a process which takes place daily, on all levels, in all sorts of workplaces. Very often, unionists make a deal with their bosses on an informal basis, after representations from a shop steward. In the bigger, especially public sector industries, professional negotiators make deals on a more formal basis.

Sometimes, employers will put pressure on unions to accept their point of view by threatening cut backs in jobs, or by locking out employees. For trade unionists, strikes are the ultimate weapon, but there are various other kinds of action they may take which will involve less hardship for themselves.

Doing it by the book One such type of action which hurts the employer, is the work to rule, in which the worker sticks absolutely to the letter of the contract of employment. If a bus conductor, for instance, is supposed to make sure all passengers are seated, he or she might see passengers to their seats one by one. The conductor will be sticking to the rules – and also considerably delaying the bus service. Similarly, the teachers decided to end their strike in February 1986, but they continued a form of disruption by opting out of 'volun-

'While so much has been done in recent years to identify and reduce some of the prime causes of industrial conflict, the future depends on the will of managements and trade unions to resolve issues which may divide them and to develop more constructive relationships.'

ACAS leaflet Improving Industrial Relations, *1985*

# of strife?

tary duties' – like covering for sick colleagues and supervising school meals.

Or workers may institute an over-time ban, ensuring they can still draw their basic pay, while denying the employer extra labour which may be badly needed. A workers' 'go-slow' has much the same effect.

In case of breakdown . . . When collective bargaining breaks down, however, the Advisory, Conciliation and Arbitration Service, ACAS, may be called in. This is a statutory body composed of three TUC members, three CBI members and three industrial relations experts. One of its chief duties is to help solve industrial disputes by providing impartial advice. In the case of a dispute where negotiations become deadlocked, ACAS can offer the services of a conciliator who tries to find some middle ground. ACAS also has a duty to offer its conciliation services to individuals who claim their employment rights have been infringed. The conciliation officers try to find a voluntary settlement before the case reaches the stage of a tribunal.

Some agreements between employers and unions have a clause which says an arbitrator will be sent for if the two sides cannot agree. In this case, the arbitrator takes a decision for the two sides, which generally breaks the deadlock without either side having to back down and lose face.

A comparatively new development in the UK are the 'no strike' agreements in which unionists make a deal with managements that they will resolve disputes without resorting to strikes. The newspaper bosses Eddy Shah and Rupert Murdoch have this kind of agreement with their workers: 'realistic' deals say the bosses, 'coercive' arm-twisting say union opponents.

Left Only one in a hundred disputes leads to a strike, but when train drivers used their 'ultimate weapon', this Londoner required a lift to work.

> '*ACAS hopes to bring the parties to a dispute together in conciliation before a strike or lockout occurs or attitudes become entrenched.*'
>
> ACAS Annual Report, 1983

The American? dream

Amerca, the 'land of plenty', has never had an organized labour movement on the scale of that in Britain. Some historians suggest that socialist ideas fell on stony ground in a country where private property is revered, individual success is the ideal, and where British-style class distinctions are unknown.

> 'All Socialist utopias come to nothing on roast beef and apple pie.'
>
> Werner Sombart in
> Why there is no Socialism in
> the United States, *1906*

Decline and fall? Today, only 18 per cent of the American workforce belong to unions, half the membership of thirty years ago. Most of these come under the banner of the thirteen million strong AFL-CIO – American Federation of Labor and Congress of Industrial Organizations. In a recent, major report, the AFL-CIO tackled the problem of how to reverse its decline and how to change the attitude of the one hundred million non-union American workers, many of whom it sees as 'hostile' or 'indifferent' to the message of organized labour. The AFL-CIO now argues that the best way to attract new members is through achieving 'bread and butter' gains. In contrast to the more ideologically-minded trade unions in other countries, 'American-style' unionism seeks to avoid action like striking, with its attendant bad publicity. Instead, they tend to compromise with management to win practical gains. Depending on your point of view, this is either 'being realistic', or it's a 'sell-out'.

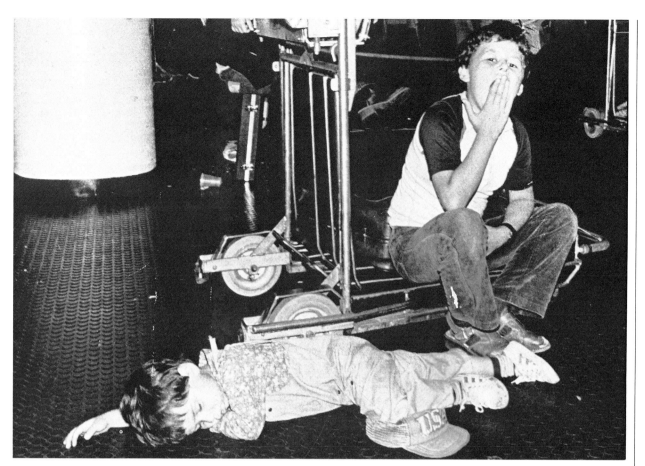

Blacklists and blacklegs Opposition to the early American unions of the 19th century was fierce. Employers exchanged blacklists of union members to prevent them from getting jobs, while factory owners employed strike-breakers and armed guards to crush strikes. States passed laws to restrict union activities, issuing injunctions against strikes and sending in troops to end disputes. The late 19th century saw a series of strikes in which government troops and strike-breakers clashed violently with unionists, leaving the unions severely weakened.

Many workers grew dissatisfied with the AFL policy of seeking benefits within the capitalist system instead of opposing it, and in the first two decades of this century, the Industrial Workers of the World (IWW) – better known as the Wobblies – organized workers to replace capitalism with socialism. Despite some notable victories, they failed to survive past the end of the 1920s.

Mob rule OK? In more recent times, scandals over Mafia infiltration and control have further undermined the American trade unions. In the late 1950s, the enormous

Teamsters' Union was one of several expelled from the AFL-CIO after charges of corruption, abusing funds, and links with organized crime. The notorious Jimmy Hoffa, the leader of the Teamsters' Union (America's biggest), survived initial purges of other corrupt leaders, but ended up in jail for defrauding the union. Eventually, he disappeared in mysterious circumstances and is thought to have been murdered.

Today, many of the American unions are still widely believed to be Mafia controlled and/or government infiltrated – hence the nickname AFL-CIA for their chief Federation!

Once he was elected, President Reagan sacked all the air traffic controllers whose strike had caused disruption at airports.

Opposite While campaigning for the Presidency in a town of high unemployment, Reagan dons a Teamsters trade union jacket.

> 'Ten thousand times has the American labor movement stumbled and bruised itself. We have been enjoined by the courts, assaulted by thugs, charged by the militia, traduced by the press, frowned upon by public opinion and deceived by politicians.'
>
> Eugene V. Debs, pioneer of US unions, 1894

Hands across the

A

s labour and trade union movements in their different forms have developed across the world, so have the international links between them. Of course there have been political and ideological problems in bringing trade unionists together, chiefly between the communist and non-communist countries. Despite attempts to reconcile their differences, the World Federation of Trade Unionists is now the biggest and pro-Soviet grouping, as distinct from the anti-Soviet International Confederation of Free Trade Unions. As employers increasingly develop their international links

sea

in the form of multinational companies, trade unionists have more and more stressed the need to balance such power by international workers' solidarity.

Solidarity action Latin American workers for instance, say they are exploited by a global economic system which concentrates wealth and power in the hands of multinational corporations at their expense. They have looked for support from fellow trade unionists in Britain and Europe, many of whom work for the same companies. British trade unionists have visited such countries to publicise cases of oppression, and at home have argued for government action against anti-union regimes. In Dublin, shop workers at Dunnes Stores went on strike to persuade their employers not to import products from South Africa, as a protest against apartheid. The British TUC, as a member of the ICFTU, is also committed to helping build trade unions in developing countries. Despite its initial hostility to membership of the EEC, the TUC now has extensive links with European trade unions.

The global village The International Labour Organization (ILO) has a membership of 151 nations, and is unique in that workers' and employers' organizations have an equal voice with those of governments in formulating policies. It aims to improve working conditions, employment prospects, education and equal opportunities for its members, while its 'Conventions' cover such matters as the right to join a trade union, the abolition of forced labour and the end of discrimination in employment.

Several hundred million workers will have been added to the world population by the end of the 1980s, say the ILO, most of them in Africa, Asia and Latin America. Yet millions of families in developing countries without the benefits of trade unions, are already missing out on the benefits of economic growth. In many of the more oppressive regimes of the Third World, trade unions are forbidden and their members' lives are at risk. Yet trade unions are often the only form of organization which exist to represent workers, and their members use them for much wider purposes than the traditional function of collective bargaining. They are often involved in running welfare and self-help schemes, like health centres, training and literacy schemes, even savings banks and loan associations.

Trade unionists across the world are pledged to help each other in times of crisis, seen here sending food to Britain's striking miners.

Opposite Many Third World workers are exploited by multinational companies, like this sheet metal worker in Panama who has no trade union to insist on safer working practices.

'Poverty anywhere constitutes a danger to prosperity everywhere.'
ILO Declaration of Philadelphia, 1944

I KRAJOWY ZJ...
DELEGATÓW N.S.Z.Z.
„SOLIDARNOŚĆ"

1981

1981

2

'Can there be many more revolting sights than the Thatchers and Reagans of the world praising Polish workers while doing everything in their power to weaken trade unions and increase unemployment in their own countries'

Denis MacShane in
Solidarity: Poland's Independent Trade Union, *1981*

In conflict with the establishment?

In many countries of the world where the people feel that they are exploited and oppressed by a powerful, ruling elite, trade unions have become a focus for change. Those who support such unions say that the only way to achieve justice and equality is to organize the workers. Those who support the governments say that these organizations are subversive, revolutionary and (usually) backed by the Soviet Union.

The other Americas Many South and Latin American countries have long been in a state of political unrest. Through coup and counter coup some have established socialist revolutions, others military dictatorships. By and large, the socialists have been backed by labour movements and trade unionists in the West, while conservative minded governments have either not backed these or have actively opposed them. In countries like Brazil, many people look to the radical trade unions to give people real control over their lives, workplaces and government institutions. A recent strike at an Avon cosmetic factory for instance, saw 1,600 workers, mostly women, holding out for an increase in their £10 a week wages, and an end to the practice of firing women who get married or become pregnant.

The United States, fearful that socialism on its borders would threaten the American way of life, has aided 'Contra' guerillas in Nicaragua to fight the government established by a workers' revolution. American multinationals based in these countries have also proved hostile to trade unions.

In some of the most oppressive of these countries – like Chile and Guatemala – workers are often tortured and killed for trade union activity which is seen as subversive. Yet the repression they encounter is taken by trade unions as a sign that their governments fear the power of the workers.

Solidarity The revolt by Polish workers in 1980 hit world headlines as it led to the creation of Solidarity, the first independent, free trade union in Soviet dominated Eastern Europe. Counting workers' families, about 80 per cent of Poles belonged to Solidarity. In the Western world, many people applauded it as an outstanding achievement of organized labour. Yet in a reversal of the usual pattern of support (as in Latin America), conservatives in the West also acclaimed Solidarity as a legitimate struggle. This was, say their critics, only because Solidarity was perceived as a threat to the Russians. Since the heady days of the strike at Gdansk shipyard however, the Polish authorities have done all they could to stop Solidarity, including the imprisonment of its leader Lech Walesa. Yet its supporters say Solidarity may be driven underground, but that 'the workers united, will never be defeated'.

Opposite Lech Walesa, leader of Poland's first free trade union Solidarity, kneels to pray with his comrades before the union's national convention.

> 'Conditions of labour exist involving such injustice, hardship and privation to large numbers of people as to produce unrest so great that the peace and harmony of the world are imperilled . . . an improvement on those conditions is urgently required.'
> ILO Constitution ILO and the World of Work, *1984*

The South African

A partheid is condemned by world opinion as a deliberate system of discrimination by a privileged White minority against the Black majority in South Africa. In the face of such pressure, the South African Government has admitted the system is outmoded and has proffered some reforms. However the Blacks say these reforms are only cosmetic, and insist on their right to true equality.

Reform or revolution? Black workers earn about a fifth of the wages of Whites in jobs like mining and manufacturing. Under the pass laws, Blacks are obliged to live apart from their families as migrant workers, and if they are 'idle' (unemployed) they are sent to the impoverished 'homelands' where children are so malnourished that a quarter of them die before their first birthday.

Until 1981, Blacks had no legal right to belong to free trade unions. Since then they have had severely restricted rights to do so, and according to the ILO, 'many leaders have been arrested, detained, tortured or banned and one died in detention'. Rank and file members have met similar treatment. Yet 1985 saw the first Congress of South African Trade Unions, COSATU, bringing 33 unions and over half a million members together. As trade unionists, they ally themselves to the political struggle for Black liberation and have pledged, through underground structures, to guide the trade union movement along the 'revolutionary course of struggle'. They are also seeking the moral and practical support of the International Trade Union Movement which has repeatedly condemned apartheid. COSATU has called for the repeal of the pass laws, the lifting of the State of Emergency, the withdrawal of troops from the townships and the release of Nelson Mandela, imprisoned leader of the African National Congress, the Black opposition party banned by the government.

A deepening crisis? However four million Black workers, many in rural areas, are not unionized and few black women have union protection. A new union for Domestic Workers, SADWA, is now campaigning for the million Black women who can expect to work 12 hours a day every day for about £5 a week. Most have to support families on this wage.

Poor Whites in South Africa are also experiencing hardship as the crisis deepens, but for the most part they seem to fear and oppose the demands of Blacks as a further

Opposite South Africa's Black workers join in the COSATU union confederation, defying the apartheid system as they demand their human rights.

Miners are bussed home after their Anglo-American bosses respond to strikes by sacking 14,400 of them, the biggest mass sacking in South Africa's history.

struggle

'South Africa's future lies in the hands of its workers. Only they, together with the progressive people of all races, can liberate us from racial hatred, inequality, class exploitation and national oppression.'

Steven Dlamini, President of SACTU, 1985

threat to themselves, rather than joining forces with them. However, some Whites have been prominent in challenging the apartheid system. Meanwhile, President Botha says he has begun power-sharing with Coloureds and Asians and that he is 'updating' the system as fast as his White supporters will allow. The Black workers, he claims, are Communist led and will bring the country to disaster. According to the Blacks, South Africa under the apartheid regime is already a disaster and only through organizing themselves will they find freedom.

'As long as the oppressive apartheid regime exists, where the above-ground trade unionist faces detention without trial, torture and murder at the hands of the police, the occupation of their townships and the brutal strike-busting tactics of the regime and bosses, there will always be a need for the South African Congress of Trade Unions.'

SACTU Trade Union Unity, 1985

Foreign devils?

Time was when the great empires of the Far East referred to colonizing Europeans as 'foreign devils'. But the post-war period has seen these same people take on the capitalists of the West, and now it is their cars, televisions, cameras and electrical goods which colonize our home markets. Some British politicians and employers point to this as an example of what can be achieved with a willing and cooperative labour force. Many in the Labour movement however, argue that our low productivity is not the fault of our trade unions – which have a low strike record – but of low investment in industry by governments and other destructive economic measures. They say the workforce in the Far East may be compliant, but in most cases it is also low paid and exploited.

A matter of enterprise? In Japan, trade unions are 'enterprise unions' consisting of the employees of one firm, as opposed to British unions which tend to organize

'Workers appear to feel an extreme loyalty to the company, in some cases singing the company anthem each morning . . . behaviour that would seem ludicrous to the British worker.'
Cooper and Bartlett in
Industrial Relations, *1976*

workers on the basis of their craft. Many Japanese workers are employed by the same company all their working lives. Some people praise the dedication and loyalty of Japanese workers. At the Nissan car plant, which claims never to have had a strike, managers and workers alike wear the same uniforms, and workers meet in 'Quality Circles' – groups who are expected, in their own free time, to suggest ideas for improving output and quality, and for saving the company money. Though wages tend to be low by our standards, large firms are paternalistic, providing cheap housing, food and transport. In return, Japanese workers seem to put the company first, expressing fears that if they go on strike, their firm will fall behind its competitors.

No complaints? However, critics say that Japanese unions tend to be merely an extension of the company, failing to take up workers' complaints. Historically, left wing trade unionism was defeated in a bitter and violent dispute at Nissan over thirty years ago, with the backing of bankers and American authorities who feared the growth of socialist ideas in the trade unions. Some Japanese workers complain that they are expected to work extremely hard, that weekend overtime is virtually compulsory and that their wages do not match productivity gains. Critics of the Japanese system also point to the plight of the many even lower-paid, non-unionized temporary workers who back up Japanese industry without welfare benefits or pension rights.

The Manpower Services Commission advertised their new, two-year YTS with the slogan 'Watch out Japan, here comes Tracy Logan', depicting a UK school leaver. However teachers argue that Japan's success is based on full-time, broad-based schooling up to the age of 18 for 90 per cent of its youth. In contrast to Britain, over a third of Japanese school leavers go on to higher education. Japanese investment and planning is also said to be superior to that in Britain.

ACHIEVE MORE
LEAD STRONGLY INNOVATE! GO FASTER

'Those who truly love their union love their company.'
Nissan union motto, 1986

Do unions create unemployment?

U

nions are often blamed for unemployment. It is said that strikes in the UK have not only damaged productivity, but have alienated foreign investors and buyers who can't rely on our output. Unions have also been blamed for causing stagnation by resisting new technology in order to protect existing jobs. Employers and the media often complain about the 'closed shop' system which prohibits non-union members from taking certain jobs. Unions are accused of demanding such high wages that employers can't afford to take on more workers. Critics say that the demands of unions hamper industry with unacceptable restraints, distorting prices and so creating further unemployment. They point to the comparatively low productivity of the British workers: some people, they suggest, would rather draw the dole than work.

Disputing the 'myths' The trade unions however, fervently disagree with their 'bad press' and see unemployment in the wider context of the country's economic problems. They blame the low levels of investment into British industry as compared with the high levels of our competitors like Japan and Germany. They say no one would rather exist on the dole than work, but productivity is low because of the poor and outdated tools of our industry. The unions also deny that lower wages mean more jobs. Our wages are amongst the lowest in Europe which they say means less money to spend on UK goods. And strikes, in spite of myths to the contrary, are at their lowest level for years.

The real villain, say the unions, is the government: by curbing the money supply and keeping up interest rates it has forced firms to cut back on production. Government cuts in public spending, they believe, have further denied contracts to business and caused many redundancies. They deny they are opposed to new technology *per se*, but do want some say over how it is introduced. Even the CBI says the union attitudes are rarely a 'constraining factor' here.

Printworkers and journalists outside the Wapping plant ask a lorry driver not to cross their picket line – a golden rule of trade unionism.

'Fortress Wapping' became the 1986 symbol of bad management as newspaper baron Rupert Murdoch kept unionists out of (or journalists inside?) his new printing plant with fences and barbed wire.

On the Street of Shame Yet new technology is causing radical changes in any kind of work which involves machines. Whole production lines have been automated and office work taken over by computers. It is feared that even our unemployment rate could be trebled if the new tech revolution is not carefully monitored.

Nowhere have the changes been more dramatic than in Fleet Street, where newspaper proprietor Rupert Murdoch (owner of the *Sun, Times* and others) sacked 5,000 striking print workers and set up a new 'high tech' plant behind barbed wire in what became known as 'Fortress Wapping'.

Was he high-handed and greedy, or were the unions intransigent and defying progress? It is a historic struggle, in which the future of many unionists hangs in the balance.

Jobs, not

Many people who work in the armaments industry, depend on the government to keep putting money into defence if they are to keep their jobs. And military spending is the biggest item on the budget, about £300 for every person in the country.

> *'The case for a British nuclear force remains as strong as ever. If war threatened in Europe, it is possible the Americans would hesitate before committing their own forces, or even opt out altogether.'* Today *editorial, 1986*

This is nearly three times what the government spends on trade, industry, energy and employment put together. In contrast to the cuts in public services like housing and education, arms spending is going up yearly.

Defending defence This makes the Ministry of Defence one of Britain's biggest

employers with over a million people working as a result of military spending. MoD does business with over 10,000 British companies. Defence accounts for some half of the output of the British aerospace industry and a third of the output of the entire UK electronics industry. Furthermore, the pro-defence lobby argue, the high level of technological expertise required in weapons research has valuable civilian spin-offs, like nuclear-generated electricity, satellite communications, the laser and computers.

Trade unionists connect our high unemployment with high government spending on arms, as this TGWU cartoon shows.

LIKE TO CHANGE PLACES?

UNEMPLOYED DEPLOYED

bombs?

Attacking defence Yet many people say that military spending damages the economy and costs us jobs. Trade unionists say that for every ten jobs created in defence, the same amount of investment could instead create 13 in the NHS or 15 in local government. The more a country spends on arms they argue, the less it spends on investment into industry. We have one of the highest rates of military spending and one of the lowest of investment: the reverse is true of our competitors like Japan. The unions also point out that while more and

more technological skill is needed in the defence field, less people are required, making employment in the arms industry insecure.

Ultimately, many unionists see military spending as a major factor in our economic

> 'We are not safe while the world sits astride a massive nuclear time bomb . . . Nor are we secure while our economy is bankrupted by excessive military spending, which pushes up unemployment and destroys our competitiveness.' *Moss Evans in* A Better Future for Defence Jobs, *1983*

decline, siphoning off valuable people and resources into a product which can only destroy. Our best scientific and managerial brains, they say, are needed – not for weapons – but for new ideas and products in industry.

Britain's biggest union, the TGWU, has a commitment to 'arms conversion' through which the defence industry would be converted to socially useful production. The resources which now make tanks could instead make medical screening systems, agricultural equipment, even brewing equipment, while maintaining thousands of defence workers' jobs.

Some say the unions should stick to negotiating wages and conditions for their members, instead of meddling in matters of international security. They differ sharply from the trade unionists who believe that the threat of nuclear war is linked to the reality of mass unemployment, and that it is within their power to contribute to the solutions to both problems.

Left In 1958 crowds gathered to protest against nuclear weapons – just as they do today in Trafalgar Square.

A clean environment?

According to trade unionists, for the first time in decades the standards of health and safety at work are declining. They say that between 1980 and 1984 the rate of fatal accidents and serious injuries reversed its long term improvement and went up by more than 25 per cent. In the past 7 years the GMBATU has investigated what it calls cases of 'gross risk' perpetuated by some of our biggest and most responsible firms, including the chemical, plastics, rubber, nuclear, asbestos and water industries. Unionists say that conditions in the smaller, non-unionized businesses are even worse than in the big ones, yet these will rarely, if ever, be visited by a Health and Safety inspector.

The employers' organization, the CBI, however, say there has been a 'steady reduction' in the numbers of accidents at work, from levels that already compared well with our overseas competitors in industry. Meanwhile the government is moving to 'liberate' small firms from what they see as the expensive and restrictive health and safety laws. The unions deplore this policy, predicting that as firms compete to cut costs in health and safety, the level of accidents at work will rise again.

Is enough being done? The Health and Safety at Work Act of 1974 set out new laws for protecting workers and the public. Under the Act, workers are obliged to be careful and to obey safety rules, while unions have a responsibility to provide health and safety representatives and to pressurize management to make equipment and work practices safer. Employers also have a legal obligation to reduce risks and hazards and to cooperate with union health and safety representatives.

> 'While recognizing the responsibility of companies to protect the health and safety of their employees . . . it is essential that excessive and bureaucratic regulations do not lead to lack of competitiveness.'
> CBI Southern Region, 1985

> 'The Thatcher regime will go down in history as one which managed to destroy much of the economy and the health of Britain at one and the same time.'
> GMBATU officials in letter to the Guardian, 1986

A mother and child wait for medical help after the poisonous gas leak from the Bhopal pesticide plant in India which killed over 2,000 people.

Opposite Smoke billows from Scunthorpe's Flixborough chemical plant after an explosion which killed several people and damaged nearby homes.

Accidents will happen . . . Trade unionists are also concerned with the wider ecological and environmental aspects of health and safety. A series of major industrial accidents in recent years – like those at Three Mile Island nuclear power station in USA in 1979 and the Bhopal chemical plant in India in 1984 – devastated whole communities. Evidence that multinational firms are less concerned for the safety of their workers in the Third World than for those in the West outraged international opinion. As a result many unions in the UK today see their role as contributing to the greater cleanliness of the environment, and protection of the community from pollution. Hence the unions' obstruction of the government's plans to dump nuclear waste at sea: NUS seamen have refused to carry the nuclear cargoes.

Yet the cost of cleaning up industry can be high. This is the reason Britain has given for its refusal to cooperate in cutting down levels of pollutants from factory chimneys which eventually fall as acid rain, destroying European lakes and forests.

A living

Whether you use the government's official poverty line of Supplementary Benefit for a family, or the TUC's figure of two-third's of average pay, there is broad agreement that anyone earning less than £100 a week is low paid. This means that more than a third of the adult workforce in the UK is low paid. Over two-thirds of the low paid are women, but young people and ethnic minorities are also vulnerable. Almost every area of work – from catering to factories, from the NHS to farming – has people earning poverty wages.

Who is to blame? The unions say that if you don't earn, you can't buy goods, and so the jobs of those making the goods are lost.

They argue that the government is making low pay worse by abolishing the Fair Wages Resolution, which once ensured fair pay for workers in private industry. They say privatisation has also led to contractors cutting costs by cutting wages, and they criticize the government's own strict pay limits for low paid workers in the NHS. Under the Young Workers scheme too, firms get a government subsidy only if they are paying low wages to the young people they take on. Our government has been criticized by the Council of Europe for not meeting their 'decent wage' target.

Meanwhile the government is weakening the powers of Wages Councils which set legal minimum rates of pay, and half a

Dinner lady leader Lil Stevens of NUPE with her colleagues: women's work is often badly paid.

'Low pay is an evil afflicting 7 million people – among women, young people and ethnic minority workers especially.'

Larry Smith, TGWU, in Living Wage, *1985*

wage?

million young people under the age of 21 no longer have their protection. To do this the government has withdrawn from the ILO Convention on minimum wages.

Cutting the cost? The government argues that, especially for young people, lower pay means more jobs. They say that scrapping the Wages Councils will enable bosses to pay the wages of up to 100,000 more young people.

Trade unionists say that these new jobs for youth are at the expense of adults, and once youngsters are old enough for adult rates, employers will sack them. Low pay, say the unions, also results in industrial waste and economic inefficiency, as firms who pay cheap rates have little incentive to train staff or invest in more productive techniques. For the first time, in 1985 the TUC voted for a national minimum wage, a policy which ties into the Labour Party's decision to adopt a statutory minimum wage.

There was an outcry when Mrs Thatcher increased her 'Top people's' (ie judges and generals) pay by up to thirty per cent. Under the Conservatives, argue their critics, the rich have got richer and the poor poorer. But in Conservative philosophy, high pay must be the incentive and reward for hard work. If we all got paid the same, they say, no one would be motivated to make any effort.

These High Court judges may earn as much in a month as low paid workers do in a year, but their salaries are only a fraction of what big businessmen may earn.

'Soaring pay rises are needed for the rich, while it's the red light for increases to the low paid according to Mrs Thatcher.'

TGWU publication Living Wage, *1985*

The forgotten generation?

In the past five years youth unemployment has roughly doubled, and in some parts of the country a quarter of school leavers have no jobs. The pay of young people has also fallen sharply behind, with pay rises about a quarter lower than those of adults. The government points out that there was a bulge in the birthrate during the 1960s so that more teenagers than usual have come on to the job market. They also say that in a recession, firms stop recruiting and those who do want new

> '**Half of all sixteen-year-old school leavers don't get jobs because the jobs aren't there.**'
> *Norman Willis, TUC, 1985*

workers want people with skills. According to the Conservative Party, their policies are designed to create the conditions in which firms will expand and create new jobs, so taking on trainees and apprentices.

Young and talented Their response has been to set up various schemes under the Manpower Services Commission (MSC) to help young people get work experience and to develop skills. The newly expanded two-year Youth Training Scheme, for instance, provides half a million places for young people, which the government says brings us more into line with our competitors, like the Japanese. They claim that two thirds of those who do YTS go on to jobs or

further education or training. 'Unemployment should not be an option' for young people said Mrs Thatcher, in defence of her job creation minister Lord Young when he removed benefits for under-18s.

Young, talented and broke? Both the TUC and the employers organization the CBI, have representatives on the MSC to consult on the running of the YTS. The unions support YTS, but on the basis that its problems must be sorted out and that good training must be ensured.

But some trade unionists say YTS is 'slave labour', that the 'wage' of about £30 paid to young people is derisory, and that employers use it to exploit cheap labour without giving proper training. There has been concern that YTS workers are more likely to be killed or maimed at work than workers generally, because of slack health and safety measures. The government also stands accused of trying to hide the true extent of youth unemployment by forcing young people on to YTS with the threat of withdrawing their benefits. Government cuts in education spending and student grants have also come under attack.

For their part, the trade unions say they offer protection against poor quality training, poor health and safety, and exploitation by unscrupulous employers. Unions can negotiate topping up the YTS allowance as well as the other usual benefits.

The unions have taken a stand against

low pay, against the threat to Wages Councils, and in their work for better pay and conditions, claim they champion the cause of equality for young people. They have an annual youth conference with young delegates and run courses for young trade unionists. They also say that they are changing their structures and ways of operating to encourage less experienced and younger members. The unions say that in the cold climate of youth unemployment,

young people need unions. They also know that they need young people.

> '*One of the reasons for unemployment amongst the under 25s is the high level of wages they have come to expect.*'
>
> Peter Morrison, former
> Conservative Employment Minister, 1985

Equal

Women in the UK are nearly half of the paid workforce (not to mention their unpaid work), yet they earn roughly a quarter less than men. They tend to work in the low status, low paid areas, like the service industries and the health service, while only a small minority ever reach the highly paid echelons of senior management. An increasing number of women work part-time and so lack many of the benefits of full time workers. This also makes it harder to unionize women. Trade unionists say they champion women's rights against sexism and exploitation. Yet women have complained they meet these very obstacles within the trade unions.

A woman's place? Since the war, the number of women in trade unions has increased until almost a third of trade unionists are women. Many unions have special women's officers and committees, and the TUC General Council has six out of fifty seats reserved for women. There is also an annual Women's TUC, but this is relatively powerless. However the position of women

'The day is still far off when working women will everywhere be equal partners with men in the efforts to achieve economic and social progress.'

World Labour Report, ILO, 1985

in trade unions often seems to mirror the position of women in society. For instance, an overwhelmingly female union like the Royal College of Nursing is run by a male General Secretary and mostly male officials.

Many things seem to hold women back from full participation in trade unions, like the 'double shift' of paid job followed by housework that leaves women without spare time, and the ties of minding children.

Those women who do reach senior positions tend to be childless, or say they have very sympathetic husbands.

Male oriented Some women say they find union meetings male dominated and off-putting and that times and venues of meetings take no account of their childcare responsibilities. In recent years, male trade unionists have been confronted with their own sexism by female members, and although they say they are making changes, a glance at most trade union conferences still reveals a sea of grey suits and balding

Right Women say that men must recognize the value of domestic work and child-care before equality is possible.

opportunity?

heads. On the other hand, unionists claim to have supported women's rights in many practical ways. They have argued for a woman's right to paid employment at a time when cuts in social services and unemployment are putting pressure on women to stay at home. They have fought – in courts and tribunals – for equal job and promotion opportunities, for decent maternity rights and for equal rights when working part-time. And in 1979 when women were campaigning for the right to choose over abortion, the TUC organized a march in their support, arguing that such a broad social issue was fundamental to women's role as workers.

In the 80s unions began to take up the issue of sexual harrassment at work, arguing that a high proportion of women workers are put under stress as a result of sexist comments, 'jokes' and even demands for sexual favours from male colleagues and bosses. The trade unions have also given their backing to the Equal Pay Act and the Sex Discrimination Act which in the 70s led to a narrowing of the gap between men's and women's pay, a trend which has now been reversed.

Women in the labour movement meet to campaign for their rights.

'I already do two jobs – I'm a worker and a mother. Now you are saying I should do three jobs and be a shop steward as well.'

June, APEX worker, 1982

'Trade unions do not always concern themselves adequately with issues important to women, such as better maternity protection and expanded child-care facilities. Equal pay has not received strong and active support from trade unions everywhere.'

Report to the 71st International Labour Conference

A sisterhood of women?

While women are generally poorer than men, Black and Third World women are the poorest of all – and the poorer women are, the more work they have to do. The UN estimates that women do two-thirds of the world's work, receive only five per cent of the world's income, and own less than one per cent of the world's wealth. What then is the role of the world's trade unions in helping women achieve equality?

A woman's work is never done The proportion of women workers who belong to trade unions varies greatly from country to country. In Asia, Africa and Latin America, women tend not to be in trade unions. In contrast, Eastern European women are half the union membership and in the USSR they are more than half. However, as in the UK, the numbers of women involved is misleading, as few women hold high leadership posts and women's needs are rarely given priority. According to the International Labour Conference there is a lack of awareness and an unwillingness on the part of men to deal with sexual discrimination, and to promote genuine equality.

Yet non-unionized women, particularly in the developing world, belong to various kinds of women's groups which give them some collective strength. The tradition of working together and helping each other has been adapted by women as the basis for trade union type organizations.

Much of women's work is invisible and unpaid – like childcare and housework – and it often goes unrecognized by trade unions and governments alike. Only in 1985 did the UN recognize that women's unwaged work – estimated in some countries to produce half of the wealth – should be counted in the GNP (gross national product) of a country. One estimate puts the value of

a British housewife's work at £320 per week.

Women's work also tends to be done in the isolation of the home or within a family unit, which makes the task of organizing a union harder. These are issues, many people argue, that the trade union movement, both at home and internationally, has yet to tackle. In the UK, women provide the cheapest available pool of labour as 'homeworkers', accepting piece work that can be done at home, and as workers in the 'Sweatshops' which often employ black and immigrant women in conditions no union would accept.

In the Soviet Union, trade unions failed to stop women's work from being system-

atically undervalued. In the West, most doctors are men and highly paid, but in the USSR they are women and (arguably, because they are women) poorly paid.

Historically, women have been accused of undermining union strength by trying to stop their menfolk from striking, fearing the effect of strikes on children and family life. On the other hand, male trade unionists have been accused of hostility to women workers, whom they fear will undercut them or take their jobs. Women have been kept out of many unions in the past by male unionists. Today however, the picture is changing. The NUM for one acknowledges that the miners' strike would have been defeated much sooner were it not for the support of the women's groups. Increasingly it seems that women and trade unions are deciding that they need each other.

Opposite (top) Low paid female labour in the Third World enables many a multinational company to make huge profits.

Opposite (bottom) These African women at market may not belong to a trade union, but women produce two-thirds of Africa's food and have their own forms of collective organization.

55

In search of the

Millions of workers – 12 million in Europe alone – earn their living abroad as migrants. Many others settle to become immigrants in their new place of work. Black and ethnic minorities are now an integral part of the British population. One school of thought argues that the predominantly White western countries exploit and discriminate against these groups, who are often without union protection. They say that racism is built into our national institutions and is responsible for great social deprivation, injustice and tension of the kind that leads to inner city riots.

Others would argue that the richer nations are doing the poorer citizens of the world a favour by allowing them within our borders. They claim that these groups are a threat to their jobs, undercutting union rates and (as in the Grunwicks dispute) working in non-unionized firms.

This Turkish 'guest worker' in Dusseldorf, Germany, is one of millions of migrant workers in Europe; here, he is consulting a trade union official.

Home is where the heart is? Much of the UK's Black and ethnic minorities arrived here in response to British Government needs to supplement the labour force in the rebuilding programme which followed the war. Many soon found themselves working for low wages in bad conditions. More recent immigrant workers – like Philippino women – still tend to work long hours for very low pay as cleaners or domestics.

Elsewhere in Europe, some industries are run by low paid migrant workers. Germany's 'gastarbeiters' or guest workers are often Turkish men who send pay home to their families. These groups remain largely unassimilated and are such a target for racial attack that a recent European Parliament report warned of the rise in fascism and racism in Europe.

In the US, Black citizens are amongst the poorest, while the economy of California depends on cheap Mexican labour. While many Mexicans do fruit picking and laundry work – which Americans won't do – they are still accused of stealing jobs, and are forced to live below the poverty line under constant threat of deportation. Hence the activities of Cesar Chavez, who established the United Farm Workers of America, a trade union for migrant and farm workers.

> 'For many countries the migrant worker is a valuable source of manpower . . . Without him or her, economic and technical progress would be slowed down.'
> The ILO and the World of Work, *1984*

promised land?

The government encouraged many Black and ethnic minority workers to help rebuild Britain in the post-war years.

Black and British In Britain it is three times harder for Black school leavers to get jobs than for Whites, and Black unemployment is double that of the country as a whole. The trade unions say that racism is a way of dividing the working class against itself which can only benefit the ruling class. The TUC has a charter against racism and individual unions have campaigned against unjust deportations and discrimination at work.

'Foreign workers meet with considerable difficulties in finding housing, bringing their families with them, and even in finding the right kind of work. Linguistic problems and xenophobia aggravate their isolation.'
The ILO and the World of Work, *1984*

What's in it for

Opposite These South
Wales miners in Merthyr
share comradeship as
workers and trade unionists.

In a time of high unemployment, many members see their unions as their best chance of job security, as a source of support from fellow workers and even as an ally in their struggle for a better way of life. Others however, see no point in joining. So what do they have to offer their members?

A friend in need? Unions can provide a whole range of very practical benefits – from strike pay to funeral allowances, insurance and even mortgage services in some cases. If you have problems at work they can provide legal advice, and should represent your interests if you encounter difficulties or disputes.

Through their union, workers can have a say in what is happening at their place of work, including their wages, the hours they work and their holidays. Unions also aim to improve the working environment, through such practical matters as better ventilation or lighting. They have a right and a responsibility to protect the health and safety of workers with the cooperation of management. And they are expected to strive for equal opportunities in jobs, training and promotion. The unions also play a wider role in seeking to influence government policy on a range of issues from unemployment to social services. They can have a powerful impact on public opinion in de-

Some people wouldn't be
interested in this NALGO
meeting in Tooting, London;
others believe such
meetings are the grassroots
of freedom and democracy.

me?

bates over the health service, pensions, education, transport and youth training, to name but a few. They see themselves as representing the views of the average working person. Yet their critics say they are undemocratic representing no one but the power hungry 'barons' who dominate them.

To join, or not to join? Depending on your job, it's your choice. Unions can insist that only members of a particular union will be allowed to work in a certain factory or office – or an arrangement called the 'closed shop'. In a 'pre-entry' closed shop you are obliged to join the union before applying for the job, as opposed to 'post-entry' membership once you have been given a job. Its advocates say this protects union strength; its critics say the closed shop is a restriction which prices other workers out of a job while protecting the interests of a few.

The cost of union membership depends on which union you join and how much you are paid, but the average fee is about 30p a week, often with special rates for youth and the unemployed. The money is usually collected monthly and paid into the branch by the shop steward, who is the elected spokesperson of the union members. The shop steward speaks for union members in joint decisions and individual problems. This is usually unpaid work which is done concurrently with his or her normal job.

It is up to you to attend meetings where you have the opportunity to discuss and vote on the policy of your union. If meetings are in working hours, you are entitled to time off to attend.

Whether they are working quietly in the background or attracting national attention through disputes, trade unions daily have a vital impact on our way of life.

Reference

Glossary

AUEW Amalgamated Union of Engineering Workers: 1,000,883 members, including engineers, foundry workers and steel constructors.

AUEW/TASS Amalgamated Union of Engineering Workers/Technical Administrative and Supervisors Section: 220,000 members including engineering draughtsmen, white collar and managerial workers in engineering and shipbuilding.

APEX Association of Professional, Executive, Clerical and Computer Staff: 98,846 members including white collar and clerical workers.

ASLEF Associated Society of Locomotive Engineers and Firemen: 22,835 members including railway drivers on British Rail and London Transport.

ASTMS Association of Scientific, Technical and Managerial Staffs: 390,000 members.

BIFU Banking Insurance and Finance Union: 154,579 members. All grades of white collar workers in banking, finance and insurance.

CPSA Civil and Public Services Association: 149,782 members including lower grades of the civil service and DHSS officials.

CSU Civil Service Union: 35,037 members. Cleaning staff in civil service offices, plus radio operators (as at GCHQ) and customs officials.

COHSE Confederation of Health Service Employees: 214,321 members. All NHS staff from porters to nurses and junior/trainee doctors and ambulance drivers.

EEPTU Electrical, Electronic, Telecommunications and Plumbing Union: 355,000 members who are electricians, plumbers, electrical goods makers etc.

GMBATU General, Municipal and Boilermakers, and Allied Trades Union: 846,565 members in local government, water and gas workers, boilermakers and shipbuilders.

IPCS Institution of Professional Civil Servants: 90,242 members in the senior ranks of the civil service and scientists in government service.

ISTC The Iron and Steel Trades Confederation: 79,082 members who are steelmakers, iron makers (rather than producers of metal goods).

NALGO National and Local Government Officers Association: 766,390 members at all levels of office based local-government workers, including social workers, town hall workers etc.

NAS/UWT National Association of Schoolmasters/Union of Women Teachers: 126,435 members. Teachers in school-based education.

NGA National Graphical Association: 126,267 members who are typesetters, blockmakers and printers.

NUM National Union of Mineworkers: 200,000 members who are face and surface workers within the mining industry.

NUPE National Union of Public Employees: 673,445 members. All NHS staff from porters to nurses, ambulance drivers, plus other local government workers such as dustmen, drivers etc.

NUR National Union of Railwaymen: 136,315 members. Railway guards, porters and drivers on London Transport.

NUT National Union of Teachers: 214,361 school teachers.

SOGAT Society of Graphical and Allied Trades: 210,462 members. Printers, board makers, paper and board product makers.

TGWU Transport and General Workers Union: 1,490,555 members. Britain's biggest union including dockers, bus and lorry drivers, airport, factory and white collar workers, car builders, agricultural workers, dyers, bleachers etc.

UCW Union of Communication Workers: 195,374 members who are Post Office workers.

UCATT Union of Construction, Allied Trades and Technicians: 249,961 members who are all types of building trades workers from brickies to plasterers, labourers to foremen.

USDAW Union of Shop, Distributive and Allied Workers: 392,307 members. Shop workers (counter and stores/offices), food and clothing and soft drink delivery drivers, some food factory workers.

Useful resources

ACAS Advisory, Conciliation and Arbitration Service, 11–12 St James's Square, London SW1Y 4LA (01-214 6000). Duties include improving industrial relations and providing the services its name suggests.

BYC British Youth Council, 57 Chalton Street, London NW11 1HU (01-387 7559/5882). A national forum for young people funded by the Department of Education and Science to promote political education and produce publications – like the 'Young Worker' pack.

CBI Confederation of British Industry, 103 New Oxford Street, London WC1A 1DU (01-379 7400). Representing the business community to government, civil service and the media as well as providing information and research services for its members.

CRE Commission for Racial Equality, Elliot House, 10–12 Allington Street, London SW1E 5EH (01-828 7022). Works for equality of opportunity and an end to racial discrimination, and also undertakes educational work.

CTU Conservative Trade Unionists, 32 Smith Square, London SW1P 3HH. Organization of trade unionists who are Conservative party supporters, producing CTU News and other political materials.

EOC Equal Opportunities Commission, Overseas House, Quay Street, Manchester M3 3HN (061-833 9244). Seeks to eliminate discrimination between men and women, for instance taking cases to tribunal courts.

HSC Health and Safety Commission, Regina House, 259 Old Marylebone Road, London NW1 5RR (01-723 1262). Responsible for securing health, safety and welfare of people at work and for protecting the public against risks arising from the work situation.

IoD Institute of Directors, 116 Pall Mall, London SW1Y 5ED. Right wing business organization which lobbies and campaigns for its members.

ILO International Labour Organization, CH 1211 Geneva 22, Switzerland.
London Office: 96–98 Marsham Street, London SW1P 4LY (01-828 6401). A UN agency which seeks to promote social justice internationally by promoting humane conditions of work.

LPU Low Pay Unit, 9 Upper Berkeley Street, London W1H 8BY (01-262 7278/9). Campaigning body for the low paid, producing many publications and information leaflets as well as exhibitions and posters.

MSC Manpower Services Commission, Moorfoot, Sheffield S1 4PQ (0742 753275). Overseas national training issues, such as providing training for school leavers through YTS.

NEDC National Economic Development Council, Millbank Tower, Millbank, London SW1P 4QX (01-211 3000). Concerned with the growth and development of the national economy.

SACTU South African Congress of Trades Unions, London Office: 8 Flowers Mews, off Archway Close, Upper Holloway, London N19 3TB. Representing the interests of South African workers against apartheid, campaigning and publishing information.

TUC Trades Union Congress, Congress House, Great Russell Street, London WC1B 3LS. Represents 91 British trade unions with a total membership of 9,855,204 of whom 2,270,724 are women. Puts the trade unionists point of view to government and public alike. Services include a reference and photographic library at Congress House (appointment only), TUC Publications on many issues of concern to unionists, and TUC Centres for the Unemployed providing welfare rights and practical assistance.

WEA Workers Educational Association, Temple House, 9 Upper Berkeley Street, London W1H 8BY (01-402 5608/9). A national movement for adult education, running courses and providing information on, for instance, the labour movement.

Further reading

The TUC as well as most individual unions and many of the organizations listed on page 61 provide a wide range of publications and educational materials on request.

Invitation to Industrial Relations by Tom Keenoy (Basil Blackwell, 1985). A lively introduction to industrial relations for students new to the subject with many contemporary anecdotes and examples.

Let me Speak by Domitila Barrios de Chungara (Stage 1, 1978). The moving story in her own words of a Bolivian woman, wife of a tin miner and mother of seven children, who became a militant women's leader and trade union activist.

Ernest Bevin by Mark Stevens (TGWU, 1981). A pen portrait of the unskilled labourer who became a great trade union leader and world statesman.

The Right to Strike by L.J. MacFarlane (Penguin, 1981). A detailed study at an advanced level of the morality of strike action.

Year of Fire, Year of Ash, The Soweto Revolt by Baruch Hirson (Zed Press, 1979). A detailed study of the Soweto Revolt and the political implications for the Black Consciousness Movement.

Digging Deeper: Issues in the Miners' Strike by Huw Benyon (Verso, 1984). A collection of essays from the left point of view concerning the issues of the miners' strike.

Getting it Together: Women as Trade Unionists by Jenny Beale (Pluto Press 1982). A feminist analysis of trade unionism as it relates to women.

Solidarity: Poland's Independent Trade Union by Denis MacShane (Russell Press, 1981). In-depth account of the creation, growth and organization of Solidarity by a prominent journalist and trade unionist.

A History of British Trade Unionism by Henry Pelling (Macmillan, 1976). The classic text book history of trade unionism for students.

Capitalism for Beginners by Lekachman and Van Loon (Writers and Readers, 1981). Witty, concise assessment of the basics of capitalism presented as an educational comic book full of pictures, cartoons and quotes.

Industrial Relations, A Study in Conflict by Cooper and Bartlett (Heinemann, 1976). An in-depth and advanced study of the subject.

Working for Freedom (South African Trade Unions) by Luckhardt and Wall (World Council of Churches, 1981). A history of black trade union development in South Africa throughout the 1970s at a detailed level.

Index

The numbers in **bold** refer to illustrations and captions

Credits

The author and publishers would like to thank the following for their kind permission to reproduce copyright illustrations:

Andes Press Agency: 34, 54 (bottom), 56
Associated Press: 47
Financial Times: 4, 14, 28, 41 (top)
Format/Brenda Prince: cover
Les Gibbard: 44
Glaube in der Zweiten Weld: 13
Sally and Richard Greenhill: 11, 51, 52, 54 (top)
James Holmes: 16, 21 (bottom)
IDAF: 39
Mansell Collection: 6
National Museum of Labour History: 8–9
Network:
    Katalin Arkell: 35
    Barry Lewis: 41 (bottom)
    John Sturrock: 10–11, 23, 29
Photo Co-op:
    G M Cookson: 59
    Gina Glover: 48, 58
    Crispin Hughes: 43
    Monash Kessler: 22
    Julia Martin: 5
    Bill Myers: 21 (top)
    Sarah Saunders 24–5, 53
Popperfoto: 17, 25, 26, 26–7, 30–1, 32, 33, 36, 38, 44–5, 46, 49, 57
Punch: 7
Rex: 12, 18–19, 42
Alan J Wylie: 15
ZEFA: 9